Personal Narrative, Collective Pain:
Healing Trauma with Prose & Poetry

Oya Kali, MSW, MPH

ISBN: 0692551131
ISBN-13: **978-0692551134**

DEDICATION

I livicate this book to my precious daughters,
Chanti & Imani Kali
my source of strength and inspiration

I give thanks 2 all of the creative African women
who serve as my divine reflections.

I give thanks 2 my ancestors
for guiding me on the straight and narrow

I give thanks 2 my Iyami
for keeping my mind, body and spirit fertile.

I give thanks to my source,
for my connection to the Light.
Ase

CONTENTS

ACKNOWLEDGMENTS

Daughters of the Dawn Media,
My publishing company

Strong Roots Cultural Arts,
My copy editors

Chantell Patrice and Isis Imani of Blak Buttafly Designs,
My design team & image consultants

Sojourners 4 Truth African Cultural Exchange,
My fiscal sponsor

& Maroon Mountain Lodge
My home base in Ghana, West Africa

CHAPTER 1
BUILDING RESILIENCE

Introduction

Globally, Africans are emotionally assaulted as citizens of chronically racist societies. Perpetually treated as less than human in social systems, worldwide, Africans have an enormous pressure placed on them; a struggle to fit into modern reality as inferior beings. Cognitive dissonance, the tension between our empowered personal narratives and societal exclusion of Africans, results, creating unwanted imbalance. Emotional equilibrium is difficult to maintain when an individual is chronically exposed to traumatic events, such as racial discrimination, community degradation, socio-economic deprivation, and political marginalization. African women, the *Mothers of Our Nation*, bare the brunt of this unjust treatment. The high incidence of premature delivery in the African American community has been biochemically linked to chronic stressors like intergenerational poverty, institutional racism, mass incarceration, malnutrition & housing discrimination. African wombmen harbor the pain of our people, and yet very few safe spaces exist to nurture the existence of our *Mothers*.

Collective Pain & Personal Narrative: Healing Community Trauma with Prose & Poetry is a book written for African women, by an African woman, who struggles to maintain immunity to the insanity known as racism/white-supremacy. In order to restore harmony to my emotional body, I write poetry, about me, my joys, my pain and my people. I heal by

1

finding harmony inside of me and then creating it in society. I become the change I want to see in the world. A catalyst, for liberation from emotional damages cause by a racist society. This book chronicles the use of a powerful preventative medicine, poetry, the foundation of our identity— our story.

The following chapters describe in detail a creative writing workshop curriculum "*Our Womb, Our Wounds, Our World*™ Writing to Heal Trauma", which aims to mitigate the impacts of psychosocial stressors, like institutional racism, on the collective consciousness of Africans in America and throughout the Diaspora. This manuscript advocates for the use of prose and poetry as tools for processing personal pain, community trauma, and societal disdain of Africans. Prose and Poetry are powerful methods to re-author our life experience. This book serves as framework for the cultivation of resilience.

BUILDING RESILIENCE

In light of recent terrorist police attacks on the African community in America, as a public health practitioner specializing in community mental health, my response was to create 'safe' community spaces for 'processing' the collective trauma of oppressed people. The goal of this workshop curriculum is to provide theoretical frameworks and practical guidelines, for the creation of an organic support system in the global African community, in order to build resiliency.

African women, globally, are incessantly processing the demands of raising a healthy family in an unjust racist society. Racism is a traumatic experience; Africans in America are chronically exposed. Africans born in America and other European economies are recurrently traumatized, often unable to properly process the emotional weight of daily exposure to racial discrimination, for life. If we are to survive, as a global African people, we need to be resilient.

What is resilience?

Resilience is the ability of a system to manage change. When individuals interact with their environments in ways that promote wellbeing and protect them against risk factors, they are demonstrating resilience.

Resilience is "positive adaptation" within a stressful situation. Characterized as one's ability to 'bounce back' from a negative experience; *resilience* is the ability to engage life with optimism, hope and humor, despite devastating loss. Resilience is overcoming stressful situation, with "competent functioning"— emerging fortified, renwed and more resourceful. Resilience is a process, not a personality trait. Resilience is developed through mindfulness. Relaxation techniques, collective creativity, emotional processing and personal narrative are all effective tools to help people enhance their resiliency.

Curative vs. Preventative Interventions

Pscyhotherapy is a behavioral health intervention used to support individuals processing stressful events and complex emotions. Pschyotherapy is used, most often, as a curative practice. *Our* writing to heal trauma workshop promotes prevention, by building resilience. Psychoeducation, affect regulation and personal narrative are key factors in the trauma healing process and the prevention of mental health disorders.

We will use components of psychotherapy to regulate our exposure to collective trauma in the African community. *Our Womb, Our Wounds, Our World* ™ Writing to Heal Trauma workshop curriculum is based on psychological theories, designed to facilitate processing of traumatic experiences and the prevention of mental health disorders. The preceding chapters will describe the foundational theories for our educational framework, as well as, provide a detailed description of the *Our Womb, Our Wounds, Our World* ™ Writing to Heal Trauma 6 week workshop curriculum .

CHAPTER 2
POETIC OBJECTIVES, WORKSHOP GOALS

Poetry is truly a potent elixir for the healing of mind, body and soul. ~Oya Kali

The *Our Womb, Our Wounds, Our World* ™ Writing to Heal Trauma workshop series is uses the medicinal magic of lyric to support African women as they process the impacts of racism on their physical, mental, emotional and social bodies. Our theory of change is simple, by rewriting our personal narratives we have the power to restructure our existence.

Our Womb, Our Wounds, Our World ™ "Writing to Heal Trauma" workshop series is a community-based narrative-healing model designed to:

1. Prevent the development of adverse mental health outcomes in the African community by building resilience among vulnerable populations using creative writing & poetic expression.

2. Familiarize participants with theories of attachment, personal narrative, affect identification, relaxation, collective trauma, worldview, and shared story.

3. Build participants' capacity to process trauma using Cognitive-Behavioral & Narrative Therapy skills. Cultivate positive coping mechanisms.

4. Strengthen the 'narrative voice' of participants with use of personal story, prose & poetry as tools for processing collective trauma in order to heal and uplift the African community in America, the Diaspora, & the Motherland.

Behavioral Health Outcomes

The *Our Womb, Our Wounds, Our World ™Writing to Heal Trauma* Writing to Heal Trauma workshop series facilitates healing of trauma through creative writing, personal narrative, poetic expression and group discussions in a "safe space" outside of the traditional therapeutic setting. The workshop is designed to support individuals as they process heavy, complex, and painful emotions, using as tools: personal narrative, prose and poetry. In addition to creative writing techniques, additional tools from CBT therapeutic methods such as psychoeducation, relaxation techniques, affect regulation & the trauma narrative are also interwoven into the curriculum. Constructing a personal trauma narrative is a healing method employed in the Cognitive Behavioral Therapy model designed for treatment of trauma. Correspondingly, participants in the *Our Womb, Our Wounds, Our World: Writing to Heal Trauma*™ workshop series will develop their capacity to pen a personal trauma narrative thru poetic expression. Workshop participants will process personal pain, and collective trauma through shared narrative as *Mothers of our Nation*.

CHAPTER 3
FOUNDATIONAL THEORIES

A theory is a set of concepts that explain a phenomenon, with planned and predicted outcomes. The Our Womb, Our Wounds, Our World ™: Writing to Heal Trauma workshop curriculum covers 5 foundational theories, which serve as the framework for the collective exploration of personal identity and collective trauma through a creative writing process.

The following five theories serve as guiding principles for our work.

Internal Working Models: Worldview and Early Attachment

According to John Bowlby, internal working models are cognitive frameworks comprising mental representations for understanding the world, self and others. We will utilize Attachment theory to explore our internal working models, which form the basis of our identity, worldview and adult attachment patterns.

HPA Axis - Hypothalamus-Pituitary-Adrenal glands.

We will utilize the HPA Axis model to frame our discussion of "Trauma" from a scientific standpoint. We will also utilize our personal and collective experiences to define the emotional impacts of trauma on our physiological and psychological health as well as it's social impacts in our community.

BPS- Biopsychosocial model.

We will utilize the Biopsychosocial model (Womb, Wounds, World) to frame our discussion of "Self". One's experience of Self is determined by the interplay of biology, psychology and social environment.

CBT – Cognitive Behavioral Therapy.

We will utilize the Cognitive model (Thoughts, Feelings and Behavior), affect identification and regulation, relaxation techniques and trauma narrative to frame our discussion of personal /collective empowerment via narrative.

NT- Narrative Therapy

We will utilize tools from Narrative Therapy (reflective listening, re-authoring) as a foundational narrative practices for our writing process.

In the following chapters we will examine each theory and discover how they serve as catalysts for our Writing to Heal Trauma process.

With open heart, I welcome you. Let us all be ready to fully engage in our collective process—healing traumas inflicted upon our community through poetry. We are African Women Writing from our Wombs to Heal our Collective Wounds & Restructure our Worlds.

CHAPTER 4
INTERNAL WORKING MODELS

Worldview

In this chapter we challenge you to define and redefine your worldview. A worldview is a mental model of reality — a framework of ideas & attitudes about the world, life, and our existence. A 'worldview' is the basic way of interpreting reality. The beliefs, values, and behaviors of an individual, stem directly from their worldview. Worldview is one's theory of the world, used to guide existence. The foundation of our worldview is formed in early childhood, based on the quality of emotional exchanges with our primary caregivers.

Early Attachments

Our relationship with self, other adults, and social systems are patterned after our early attachments to our primary caregivers. John Bowlby and Mary Ainsworth in the late 1960s developed "attachment theory" to describe the quality of emotional exchanges between children and their caregivers. Attachment bonds between a child and a caregiver are based on the child's need for safety, security and protection.

Secure attachment and healthy psychosocial development occur when the caregiver meets the child's biopsychosocial needs. If the opposite is true, the child forms an insecure attachment to their primary caregiver, and subsequently develops poor interpersonal skills, poor self-concept, & decreased social functioning. Insecure attachment styles in early childhood often lead to the development of anxious personality traits and avoidant adult attachment styles.

Working models

Children form expectations about the accessibility and helpfulness of their caregivers. These expectations shape children's thoughts about themselves. Most especially how valued and deserving they are of good care from their caregivers. The expectations of others and beliefs about self constitute internal "working models" used to guide interpersonal functioning i.e. 'relationship' behaviors. Working models help guide behavior by allowing children to anticipate and plan for caregiver responses. Children usually interpret life experiences from the lens of their working models. Internal working models form the basis of our personal narrative as adults.

In the *Our Womb, Our Wounds, Our World*™ Writing to Heal Trauma workshop we will utilize internal working models and worldview to explore the foundation of our personal narrative.

Questions for Reflection:

1. **What is your internal working model?**
2. **Were your basic needs met as a child?**
3. **Are you distrustful in your adult relationships?**
4. **How does your internal working model influence your response to traumatic experiences?**

CHAPTER 5
TRAUMA, STRESS & HPA AXIS

Being born Black is traumatic, especially if you are proud of your melanin. _Oya Kali

What is Trauma?

Trauma is a natural response to a tragedy. Immediately after the traumatic event, typical reactions include denial, uncontrollable emotions and strained interpersonal relationships. Processing complex emotions following traumatic events can help individuals cope with their feelings, thoughts and behaviors. Writing about trauma reduces stress, aids immunity, strengthens cognitive processes, and builds resilience. In this chapter we define trauma as the excessive activation of the HPA axis.

HPA Axis: Biological models of Stress

The neurobiological basis of stress and resilience is an emerging field. Humans biologically respond to stress by activating a wide range of behavioral and physiological reactions, the stress response, located with the hypothalamic-pituitary-adrenal (HPA) axis. Corticotropin-releasing factor (CRF) plays a central role in mediating the stress response by regulating the hypothalamic-pituitary-adrenal (HPA) axis.

Corticotropin-releasing factor (CRF), the principle regulator of the HPA axis, is a 41 amino acid peptide produced in hypothalamic tissue. CRF is widely expressed throughout the central nervous system (CNS) and in a number of peripheral tissues. In the periphery, CRF has been detected in the adrenal gland, testis, placenta, gastrointestinal tract, thymus, and skin. CRF correspondingly aids the regulation of the autonomic nervous system, learning, memory, and reproduction

Released in response to stress, CRF initiates a cascade of events that culminate in the release of glucocorticoids from the adrenal cortex. Biofeedback plays a prominent role in regulating the magnitude and duration of glucocorticoid release. The biological effects of the HPA axis are usually adaptive; however, excessive activation of the HPA axis, resulting from chronic stress and unprocessed trauma, may contribute to the development of pathologies. Chronic stressors such as institutional racism damage the regulation of the HPA axis and can cause numerous psychological and physiological health problems.

The goal of this chapter is to educate readers on the maintenance of emotional homeostasis, despite adversity, using relaxation and affect regulation via prose and poetry. In the *Our Womb, Our Wounds, Our World*™ Writing to Heal Trauma workshop series we use affect identification and poetic expression to regulate our nervous system responses to trauma and emotional pain.

CHAPTER 6
BUILDING SELF AWARENESS (BPS)

Bio-Psycho-Social Model

The goal of *Our Womb, Our Wounds, Our World:* Writing to Heal Trauma™ workshop series is to rewrite our personal narrative. In order to rewrite the story of our lives, we must first understand all of the factors, which influence our daily functioning as individuals. In this chapter we will increase the self-awareness of participants by utilizing the biopsychosocial model as a theoretical framework for exploration of the component parts of our emotional health.

Drawing on the systems theory of Weiss and von Bertalanffy, psychiatrist George L. Engel first describes the biopsychosocial model as an examination of the biological, psychological (thoughts, emotions, & behaviors), and social (socio-economical, environmental, & cultural) factors, which play a significant role in optimal human functioning. Engel theorized that, health is best understood in terms of a combination of biological, psychological, and social factors rather than purely in biological terms.

The *biological* component of the biopsychosocial model seeks to examine human health based on the functioning of the individual's body.

The *psychological* component of the biopsychosocial model examines psychological causes for a health problem; such as lack of self-control; emotional disorders; and negative thinking.

The *social* component of the biopsychosocial model investigates the influence of social factors; such as socioeconomic status; culture; poverty; and technology on physical and mental health.

In essence, the biopsychosocial model examines the totality of human existence when considering risks factors that impede optimal health.

The biopsychosocial model will serve as a framework for understanding the various factors that influence our overall state of physical, mental and emotional wellbeing.

In the "Writing to Heal Trauma" workshop, participants will explore the effect of the biopsychosocial model on their cognitive models (thoughts, feelings, behaviors). Participants will use prose and poetry to assess their overall functioning as human beings, in a safe, creative, spiritually elevating, and emotionally supportive healing environment.

CHAPTER 7
COGNITIVE PROCESS & TRAUMATIC EVENTS

Cognitive Behavioral Therapy (CBT)

Cognitive behavioral therapy (CBT) is a short-term, goal-oriented psychotherapy treatment. The goal of CBT is to change patterns of thinking. CBT works by changing people's beliefs, attitudes and their behavior. CBT focuses on altering cognitive processing (thoughts, images, beliefs and attitudes) and accordingly our behavioral response to emotional triggers.

Cognitive behavioral therapy is a combination of psychotherapy and behavioral therapy. Psychotherapy highlights the importance of personal meaning and thinking patterns, which begin in childhood. Behavioral therapy pays close attention to the relationship between our problems, our behavior and our thoughts.

The specific components of Cognitive Behavioral Therapy treatment interwoven into the *Our Womb, Our Wounds, Our World* ™ curriculum are summarized by the acronym **PRACTICE**:

- **P**sychoeducation—provided to describe the impact of trauma and common reactions.
- **R**elaxation and stress management skills
- **A**ffective identification, expression and modulation are taught to help clients identify and cope with a range of emotions.
- **C**ognitive processing illustrates the relationships among thoughts, feelings and behaviors. This helps clients modify inaccurate or unhelpful thoughts about the trauma.
- **T**rauma narration, in which the client describes their personal traumatic experiences, is an important component of the CBT treatment.
- **I**n vivo mastery of trauma reminders is used to help clients overcome their avoidance of situations that remind them of the original trauma, yet are no longer dangerous.
- **C**onjoint sessions help the client talk to loved ones about the trauma.
- **E**nhancing future safety: the final phase of the treatment, addresses safety, helps the client to regain developmental momentum, and covers any other skills the client needs to end treatment.

In this chapter we learned how to utilize psychoeducation, relaxation skills, affective identification, cognitive processing, trauma narration, and the cognitive model to explore the relationship between our thoughts, feelings and behavior. *Personal Narrative, Collective Pain* is written to support African women seeking to re-author their personal narrative, redefine their worldview, and reclaim their lives.

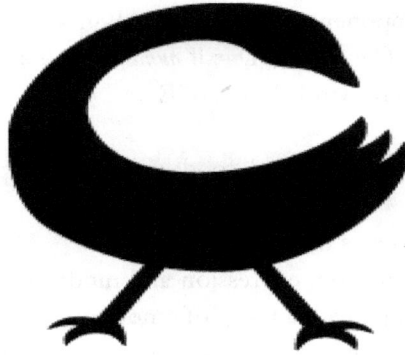

CHAPTER 8
NAVIGATING NUANCED NARRATIVES

Narrative Therapy

Our personal narrative exposes our worldview. An individual's identity is fashioned by their story of self. Personal narrative reflects the multi-storied nature of our identities. Personal narratives scaffold individuals as they redefine life's challenges: opportunities. Re-authoring personal narrative is a powerful way to reclaim our lives from problems. An individual's values, hopes, and commitments, defy the gravity of any problem. With poetry one can 're-author' their experience of life.

Problem-saturated stories often gain dominance in one's personal narration, at the expense of value laden alternative narratives, which empower the individual and build resilience. Examples of exceptions to the problem, not predicted by problem-focused narrative, are important to strengthen an alternative narrative. Alternative narratives, however, are often disqualified by dominant discourse. Subjugating narratives include capitalism; psychiatry; patriarchy; and Euro-centricity.

Externalizing Problems

Below is a guideline for assessment of a 'problem' for its effects on, or influences as, a "dominant story" in our lives.

Analyze a problem by "externalizing" it:
1. Name a problem -- *so that a person can assess its effects in his or her life,*
2. Know how it operates or works in their life,
3. Relate their earliest history to the problem,
4. Evaluate the problem,
5. Choose their relationship to it.

Method

In narrative therapy a person's values, beliefs, skills, and knowledge base help them regain their life from a problem. Narrative therapy helps clients examine, evaluate, and change their relationship to a problem by posing questions that externalize the problem to thoroughly investigate it. These questions often examine how the problem influences life, and explore exceptions to the problem's influences. This technique leads to naming an alternate direction in life.

Narrative therapy relies on the client's sources of resilience, evidenced in nearly forgotten events. Through conversation, Narrative therapy explores the influence of people who have contributed new knowledge or skills, and examines the impact they have on the client's life trajectory. Uncovering exceptions to problems provides a foundation of personal values that provide support when facing challenges; and ultimately an alternate direction in life.

Outsider witnesses

In narrative therapy, outsider witnesses are invited listeners who have their own knowledge and experience of the problem at hand. First the outsider witness listens to the client's narrative without comment. Then they are prompted to simply mention phrases or images that stood out for them, followed by any similarities between their life struggles and those just witnessed. Lastly, the witness is asked in what ways they feel a shift in how they experience themselves from when they first entered the room.

Next, the client, who has been listening to the reflections of the outsider witness, is asked to identify the images or phrases that stood out in the conversation, and the felt connections. Through this process the client acquires new knowledge, coping mechanisms and alternative directions in life. The main aim of the narrative therapy process is to collectively engage in problem solving and provide the best alternative solution.

We will utilize this therapeutic model when providing narrative reflections, and engaging all participants in the collective process of healing community trauma through prose & poetry.

CHAPTER 9
WORKSHOP OBJECTIVES & CURRICULUM

Writing to Heal Trauma

This 6 week writing series is designed to help African women heal from trauma exposure. Trauma is defined as a deeply distressing or disturbing experience.

In our "Writing to Heal Trauma" workshops, we focus on identifying & healing trauma by developing the narrative voice of those left voiceless as a result of a traumatic experience. In our workshop series we highlight the connection between our thoughts, feelings and actions to help women rewrite the stories of their life thru prose & poetry.

Our writing workshops are a safe sacred space for the processing of personal pain. We utilize writing as a tool to help process some of our most vulnerable emotions as African women. Each person will begin a journal.

By the end of the *Our Womb, Our Wounds, Our World* ™ writing experience participants will be familiar with basic psychological theories of personal narrative, affect identification, community trauma, and resilience. Participants will learn how to use personal and collective narrative to heal and uplift their community from impacts of traumatic experiences. The ultimate goal of the *Our Womb, Our Wounds, Our World* ™ Writing to Heal Trauma workshop series is to BUILD RESILIENCE in our community by creating a support system for Black women, who are constantly processing the pressures of raising a black family in an unjust racist society.

WORKSHOP CURRICULUM

Week 1
Learning Objectives

In Week 1 participants are introduced to the foundational theories and concepts for the workshop. Each participant will outline their goals and begin a discussion on Worldview (Attachment), Personal Narrative (NT), Trauma (HPA) and its impacts (BPS/CBT/Cognitive Model).

The first set of writing exercises are focused on helping participants to define self, trauma & narrative methods for coping with life stressors. Participants will discover ways to productively process pain with poetry. As well as, strengthen their muscle relaxation and affect regulation skills.

Activities

"Greetings to All Mothers Of Our Nation
We welcome you to the first "Writing to Heal Trauma" workshop."

Writing to Heal Trauma Workshop Agenda: Week 1

Intro Workshop & Facilitator (5 minutes)	Cover the workshop learning goals and objectives: Build Resilience via Poetry
Intro Participants (10 minutes)	We will all take 1 minute to share from our story of self "(check-in)
Facilitator Introduction	Story of Self, Us, Now!!
Questions / Reflections (5 minutes)	Answer clarifying questions
Intro Theoretical Models (10 minutes)	Cover the foundational theories of "Self" for our workshop series (AT, CBT, BPS, NT)
What is Trauma? (15 minutes)	Define trauma, within a theoretical framework (the HPA AXIS) and viscerally based on our personal/collective experience
Group Writing Activity	Sacred Space
Trauma & our Worldview? (10 minutes)	Examine personal & collective experiences of trauma
Group Writing Activity	Sacred Space
Closing (5 min)	Close with a Mindfulness Exercise (Deep Breathing) (Positive Affirmations)

Week 1 Writing Activity

The first writing prompt: (Brainstorm)

When you think about the word "trauma" list all of the verbs, adjectives and nouns that come to mind. Then draft 3 short 'free writes' with the following headings...

Biological:	Describe "how your body feels" in reaction to the thought of trauma.
Psychological:	What emotions come to mind, how do you feel when exposed to trauma?
Social:	What are social triggers in your world that cause you to feel traumatized?

Second Writing prompt: (Poetry writing)

When you think about the words/concepts you have listed in connection to trauma from the brainstorming activity.

Describe trauma. Use creative, abstract features to help readers visualize the monstrous effects of trauma in your life.	8 – 12 lines
How does trauma impact your womb? Womb: your physical and spiritual "center of Self"	8 – 12 lines
What emotional wounds resonate when you think about trauma/ what triggers you?	8 – 12 lines
How does trauma impact your identity in the world?	8 – 12 lines
Answer each question with 8 to 12 lines of poetry.	Participants will share their poetry during the 2nd workshop.

.

21

Week 2
Learning Objectives
In Week 2 participants are introduce to the foundational concepts for therapeutic narrative. In this session we begin our creative discussion of trauma and how it impacts our world. Participants will use narrative tools.

The first set of writing exercises is focused on helping participants to define self, trauma & life stressors. Participants will discover ways to productively process pain with poetry. As well as, strengthen their muscle relaxation and affect regulation skills.

In this session we will focus on crafting our personal narrative thru poetry.

Activities
"Greetings to All Mothers Of Our Nation
We welcome you to the second "Writing to Heal Trauma" workshop."

Writing to Heal Trauma Agenda: Week 2

Intro Workshop (5 minutes)	Cover the Workshop learning goals and objectives for the session
Check-ins (10 minutes)	Take 10 minutes to share from our story of self (check-in)
Opening Questions/Review/Reflections (5 minutes)	Answer any clarifying questions
Intro Today's Activity (5 min)	Review the writing prompt from last session.
Trauma: the impact on our Womb, Wounds, & Worldview? (30 minutes)	Share our personal & collective experience of trauma & its impact on our worldview via poetry.
Group Poetry Activity	Sacred Space
Closing (5 min)	Close with a Mindfulness Exercise (Deep Breathing & Positive Affirmations)

"Raising the Vibration of Our Nation thru Narration"

Week 3
Learning Objectives

The foundational theories and concepts for the 3rd workshop focus on the intersection of trauma and identity. Participants begin a discussion on the collective trauma of being African within a White Supremacist power structure, and the effects of this collective trauma on their personal life.

The second set of writing exercises are designed to help define the meaning of collective trauma for African descendants and identify positive methods for coping with societal stressors.

In the 3rd workshop participants discover ways to process collective pain productively. The workshop will focus on strengthening personal narrative and collective identity thru poetry & creative writing.

Activities

"Greetings to All Mothers Of Our Nation
We welcome you to the third "Writing to Heal Trauma" workshop."

Writing to Heal Trauma Agenda: Week 3

Intro Workshop (5 minutes)	Cover the Workshop learning goals and objectives for the session
Check-ins (10 minutes)	Take 10 minutes to share from our story of self (check-in)
Opening Questions/Review/Reflections (5 minutes)	Answer any clarifying questions
Intro Today's Activity (5 min)	Review the writing prompt for today's session.
Trauma and Identity: African Women in Western Society (30 minutes)	Share personal & collective experiences of trauma via discussion, prose & poetry.
{Group Writing Activity}	Sacred Space
Closing (5 min)	Close with a Mindfulness Exercise (Deep Breathing & Positive Affirmations)

Week 3 Writing Prompt
The first writing prompt: Brainstorm

Affect Identification	When you think about "trauma" in the African community, list all of the verbs, adjectives and nouns that come to mind.
Biological:	Describe how your body feels in reaction to the thought of our collective trauma.
Psychological:	What emotions come to mind? How do you feel when exposed to trauma as an African woman?
Social:	What are social triggers that cause you to feel traumatized as an African/woman? How is your identity shaped by collective trauma?

===

Second Writing prompt: Poetry writing

Using the words/concepts you have listed from the brainstorming activity on our collective trauma as Africans write 24 to 36 lines of poetry, which reflect your emotional processing of our collective trauma.

How does our collective trauma impact your womb/body?	Write 8 to 12 lines
What emotional wounds surface when you think abt. our collective trauma? What triggers you?	Write 8 to 12 lines
How does our collective trauma impact your identity in the world?	Write 8 – 12 lines

Week 4
Learning Objectives
The foundational theories and concepts for the 4th Writing to Heal Trauma workshop focus on the intersection of trauma and identity. Participants will share their personal narrative on their experience of collective trauma, being African within a White Supremacist power structure. This poetic trauma narrative focuses on the effects of collective trauma on our personal lives.

The second set of writing exercises are focused on helping participants to define collective trauma as African descendants and to identify constructive methods for effectively coping with societal stressors.

In the 4th workshop participants will process collective pain productively using poetry as narrative therapy. The 4th workshop focuses on strengthening our personal narrative and collective identity thru poetry readings.

Activities
"Greetings to All Mothers Of Our Nation
We welcome you to the fourth "Writing to Heal Trauma" workshop."

Writing to Heal Trauma Agenda: Week 4

Intro Workshop (5 minutes)	Cover the Workshop learning goals and objectives for the session
Check-ins (10 minutes)	Take 10 minutes to share from our story of self (check-in)
Opening Questions/Review/Reflections (5 minutes)	Answer any clarifying questions
Intro Today's Activity (5 min)	Review the writing prompt from last session.
Trauma: the impact on our Womb, Wounds, Worldview? (30 minutes)	Share our personal & collective experience of trauma via poetic expression.
{Group Poetry Activity}	Sacred Space
Closing (5 min)	Close with a Mindfulness Exercise (Deep Breathing & Positive Affirmations)

"Raising the Vibration of Our Nation thru Narration"

Week 5
Learning Objectives
The 5th workshop examines trauma and resilience. In this session, participants are introduced to the concepts of healing of personal and collective trauma through resilience.

The third set of writing exercises is focused on helping participants identify personal narrative as a source of resilience for self and others. In the final writing assignment participants advocate for use of prose and poetry as an effective method for coping with societal stressors.

Participants in the 5th workshop discover ways to serve as sources of resilience, capable of processing collective pain. In this workshop participants will strengthen their collective identity thru personal narrative.

Activities
Greetings to All Mothers Of Our Nation
We welcome you to the fifth "Writing to Heal Trauma" workshop.

Writing to Heal Trauma Agenda: Week 5

Intro Workshop (5 minutes)	Cover the Workshop learning goals and objectives for the session
Check-ins (10 minutes)	Take 10 minutes to share from our story of self (check-in)
Opening Questions/Review/Reflections (5 minutes)	Answer any clarifying questions
Intro Today's Activity (5 min)	Review the writing prompt for today's session.
Trauma and Resilience: African Women & Sources of Resilience (30 minutes)	Share our personal experience of resilience via discussion, prose & poetry.
{Group Writing Activity}	Sacred space
Closing (5 min)	We will close with a Mindfulness Exercise (Deep Breathing & Positive Affirmations)

Week 5: Writing Prompt
FINAL WRITING ASSIGNMENT.

Poems embody our call to action. This poem will provide discourse on the impact of trauma in our lives, advocate for use of our cultural identity as a source of resilience, and encourage others to narrate healing thru poetry.

Part 1: Who am I?
(18 to 36 lines total)

In this section of the poem we are going to describe ourselves from our highest optimal functioning, the impact of trauma on our homeostasis, and how we restore emotional equilibrium to our core being.

Who are you at your core *(internal working model)*	(2 to 6 lines)
How do feel when you are at peace? *(Affect Id)*	(2 to 4 lines)
Describe what the absence of tension feels like in your womb, your emotional body and your social environment. *(Alternative story)*	(4 to 6 lines total)
Define trauma	(2 to 4 lines)
Describe the impacts of trauma on your womb & world	(4 to 6 lines total)
Describe how you overcome the impact of trauma and return to a state of peace as an individual.	(4 to 6 lines)

==

Part 2: Who are we?
(24 to 36 lines total)

In this section of the poem you will use poetry to narrate personal & collective healing of traumatic experiences.

Describe "Self" within the context of your community.	(4 to 6 lines)
How do you define " your people" ?	(4 to 6 lines)
Describe our present 'state of existence' as Africans under oppression?	(2 to 4 lines)
Describe your identity as an African woman from a bio-psycho-social perspective	(4 to 6 lines)
Define our collective trauma	(2 to 4 lines)
Describe the impact of our collective trauma on your experience of life	(4 to 6 lines in total)
Describe your source of resilience. How do you process our collective trauma with personal narrative? How can we *Heal* as a community?	(4 to 8 lines)

Week 6
Learning Objectives
The foundational theories and concepts of the final Writing to Heal Trauma workshop are trauma and resilience. In this session participants begin their poetic expression on the healing of personal and collective trauma through resilience.

The third set of writing exercises is focused on aiding participants as they identify their personal narrative as a source of resilience for self and others. In our final writing assignment participants will advocate for use of prose and poetry as an effective coping mechanism for societal stressors.

Participants in the final workshop will discover ways to serve as sources of resilience. Poetry is a powerful tool for processing the collective pain of Africans living in an unjust society. In this final workshop participants will strengthen their collective identity & resiliency through prose and poetry.

Activities
Greetings to All Mothers Of Our Nation
We welcome you to the sixth & final *Writing to Heal Trauma* workshop.

Writing to Heal Trauma Agenda: Week 6

Intro Workshop (5 minutes)	Cover the Workshop learning goals and objectives for the session
Check-ins (10 minutes)	Take 10 minutes to share from our story of self (check-in)
Opening Questions/Review/Reflections (5 minutes)	Answer any clarifying questions
Intro Today's Activity (5 min)	Review the writing prompt from last session.
Resilience: Healing the impact of trauma on our Womb, Wounds, and Worldview? (30 minutes)	Share our personal & collective experience of trauma and sources of resilience via poetry.
{Group Poetry Activity}	Sacred Space
Closing (5 min)	Close with a Mindfulness Exercise (Deep Breathing & Positive Affirmations)

"Raising   the   Vibration   of   Our   Nation   thru   Narration"

APPENDIX A: DIAGRAMS

**Cognitive
Model**

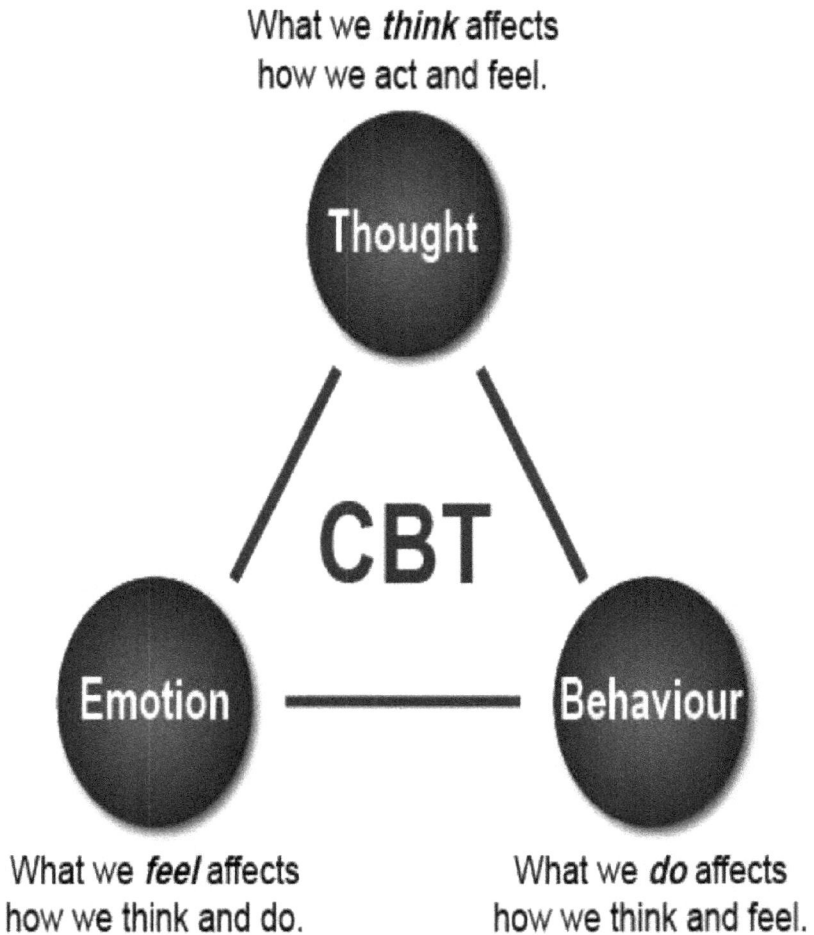

What we *think* affects
how we act and feel.

Thought

CBT

Emotion — Behaviour

What we *feel* affects
how we think and do.

What we *do* affects
how we think and feel.

Biopsychosocial Model

The biopsychosocial model of health

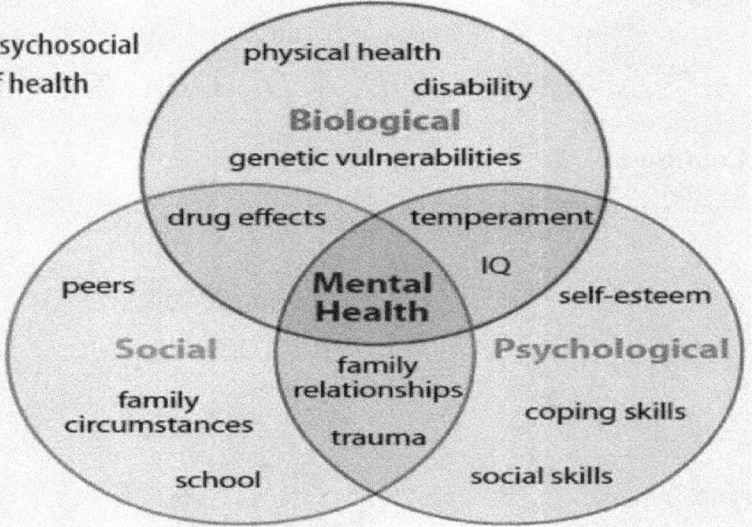

HPA Axis

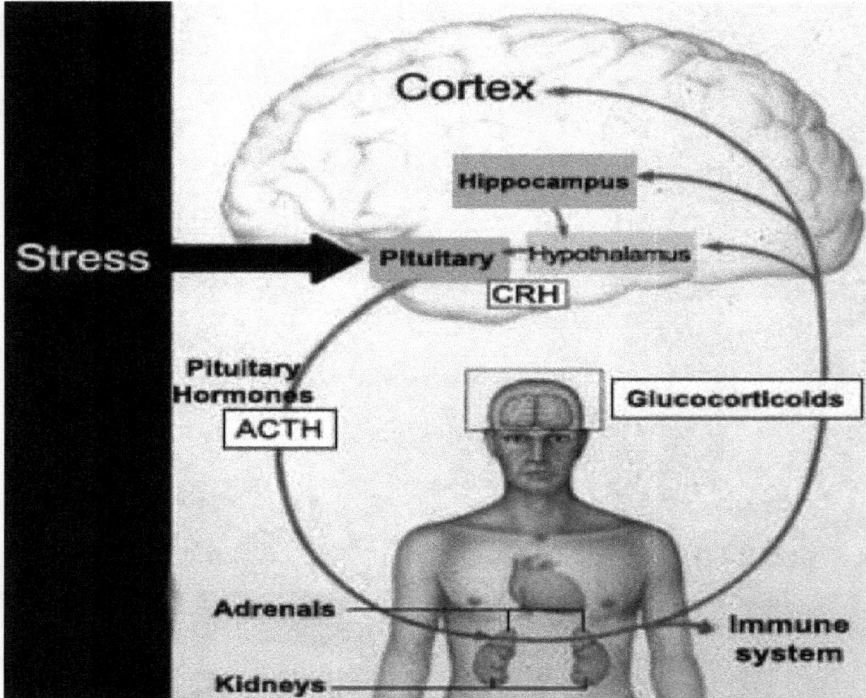

Affect Identification

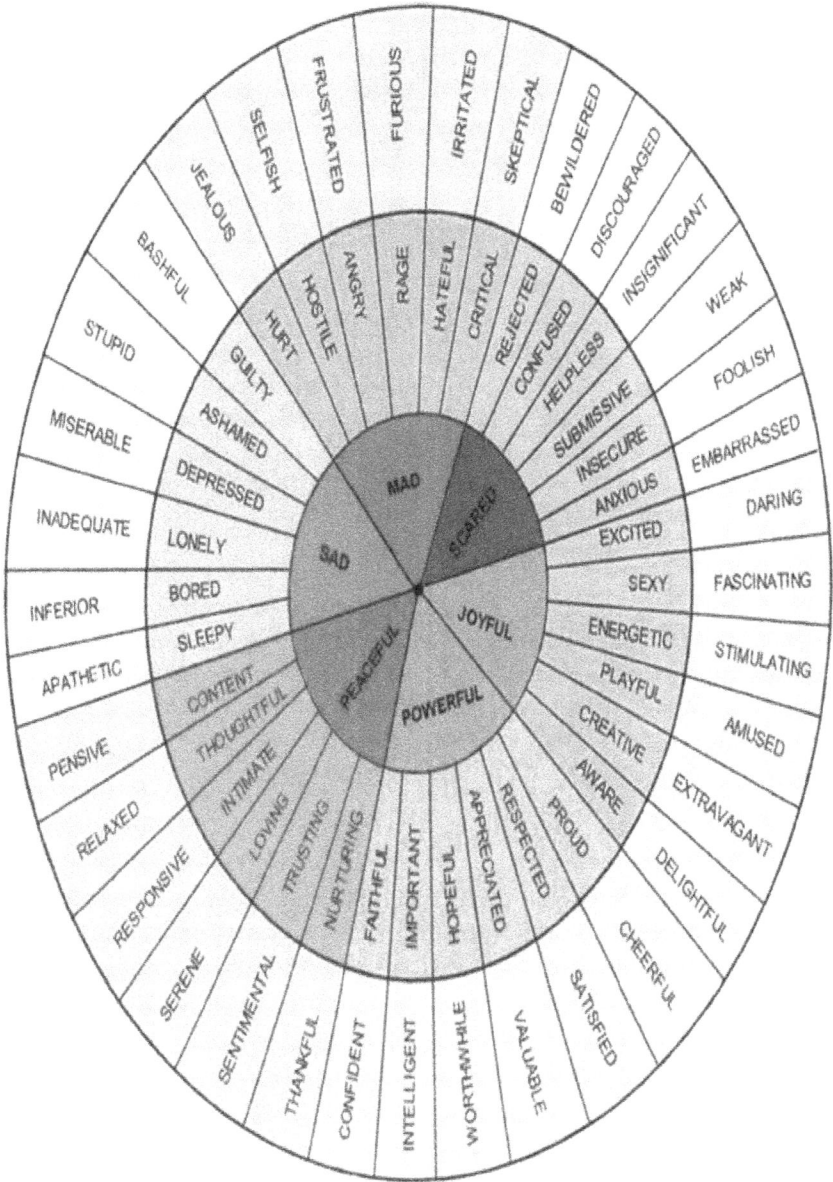

ABOUT THE AUTHOR

Oya Kali, is the author of the *Our Womb, Our Wounds, Our World* ™ Writing to Heal Trauma curriculum and lead workshop facilitator. As a public health practitioner who specializes in community mental health, Oya Kali wants to create 'safe' community spaces for African women to process their collective trauma as oppressed people. The goal of this workshop curriculum is to provide a theoretical framework and practical guidelines for creation of organic social support systems in the African community. Oya Kali's life work is building resilience.

Through this workshop series, Oya Kali hopes to offer a poetic formula to help 'her people' regulate their emotional bodies and build resilience. " It is my expressed hope that all *Our Womb, Our Wounds, Our World* ™ Writing to Heal Trauma participants will gain a stronger connection to other women in the global African community who have devised creative ways of developing and maintaining resilience in the face of great adversity"
☐
#Resilience

"Racism is a traumatic experience; Africans in America are chronically exposed. If we are to survive, as a global African people, we need to be resilient." *Oya Kali ~ Personal Narrative, Collective Pain.*
☐

www.ingramcontent.com/pod-product-compliance
Lightning Source LLC
Chambersburg PA
CBHW072212090426
42740CB00012B/2494